"NON BENE PRO TOTO
LIBERTAS VENDITUR AURO"

ISBN 953-7258-08-4

Compiled by
TANJA ŠIMUNDIĆ - BENDIĆ

Edited and designed by
MLADEN MILIĆ

Photographs by
NIKOLA VILIĆ
ANDRIJA CARLI

For the Publisher
MLADEN MILIĆ

Translated by
KREŠIMIR KUNEJ

Set and printed by
GRAFOMARK

CIP- Katalogizacija u publikaciji
Znanstvena knjižnica Zadar

UDK 908(497.5 Dubrovnik)

ŠIMUNDIĆ-Bendić, Tanja

Dubrovnik : history and culture / Tanja Šimundić-
Bendić ; <photographs by Nikola Vilić, Andrija Carli ;
translated by Krešimir Kunej> . -Zadar: Maris liber,
2005. - 96 str.: ilustr. u bojama ; 22 cm

Izv. stv. nasl.: Dubrovnik.

ISBN 953-7258-08-4

DUBROVNIK

HISTORY AND CULTURE

TANJA ŠIMUNDIĆ · BENDIĆ

MARIS LIBER

THE CITY OF STONE LACE

There are only a few places on this planet where a man feels like he has stepped into a completely different world. That is exactly how people experience Dubrovnik, a stone city whose whiteness is guarded by the 412-meter high Srđ hill on the North, and by the crystal clear sea that has islands scattered over it like pearl-shells on the South.

The city itself, compared by some to Saint Tropez from the 60-ies, is also the center of a number of historical events, a temple of cultural events that have through the epochs left their mark in all of its pores, an urban city center whose pulp still pulsates in the rhythm characteristic to itself, yet a crossroad of the ancient and the contemporary /

urban and rural ways of life as well. The city was named the Slavic name Dubrovnik after Dubrava, a dense coastal oak-tree forest that once covered the Srđ hill.

Dubrovnik is the center of the Dubrovnik-Neretva County that is located on the very South of Croatia, and with its 8171 square kilometers in area it is by size the second largest county in the category of Croatian coastal counties. This county is divided into 17 districts that consist of 188 settlements and five urban centers - Dubrovnik, Korčula, Metković, Ploče and Opuzen, and are inhabited by 126 thousand residents. According to the census from 1991, in Dubrovnik alone there were 49,728 residents.

Geographical Data

The city of Dubrovnik is situated at 42.40 degrees latitude and 18.5 degrees longitude, it is the southernmost Croatian city that has been throughout history guarded against numerous conquerors by among other things two well protected harbors -the City Harbor *(gradska luka)*, defended by guard fortifications, and the Gruška Harbor, located on the West side of the city, at the former safe anchoring location of ships that were on their way to Otrant.

Thanks to the plenty of water that came from Ombla, Gruž and Mlin, from Šumet, a spring about 13 kilometers from Dubrovnik, as well as the island of Lokum, the city has always been a safe harbor and a place at which numerous sea fearers and land travelers sought refuge and salvation. Dubrovnik can also thank the ideal climate for its ac-

Dubrovnik (City)

cessibility, it is within a markedly Mediterranean climate, there are more than 250 sunny days during a year, the mean yearly temperature amounts to 17 degrees Celsius, the average sea water temperature amounts to 21 degrees, and very mild Winters and sunny and dry Summers have always brought tourist swallows to the city, ones who desired the whole range of original Mediterranean tastes, colors and smells. When we add to this that the average temperature during the Winter amounts to 10 degrees Celsius, that winds provide a Summer refreshment breeze, that the rain season is mostly during the colder periods of the year, and that snow is in this region of Croatia an exception, it comes as no surprise that Dubrovnik has always been categorized as the true central tourist destination.

Line of Islands

The island of Pelješac, the Ston isthmus and a very narrow seaside up to Rijeka Dubrovačka on the Northwest part make the coastal area of the entire Dubrovnik region complete. The East part of this region entails the area of Dubrovnik district, the cities of Cavtat and Konavle, which at the very Southeast part ends with the Prevlaka Peninsula and the Oštro Cape at the entrance to the Bokokotorski Gulf. The southernmost Croatian county offers an array of islands and small islands starting from Korčula, Lastovo and Mljet, the Elafit island region that consists of Olipa, Jakljan, Šipan, Lopud, Koločep and Daksa, as well as Lokrum that is situated very close to the old City Harbor of Dubrovnik.

Rich Vegetation

The warm Mediterranean climate is the main factor of the development of rich and various vegetation that consists of - along with the indigenous flora- specimens of sub-tropical and at some places also continental plants. Arboretums and numerous gardens, some preserved even today, lemon and orange trees, aloe and palm trees, as well as exotic plants that captains and sea-fearers of Dubrovnik brought from their journeys have created a splash of colors and smells that are recognizable and preserved to this day.

The City Harbor and the St. Ivan Fortress

THE HISTORY OF THE CITY

The Laus Peninsula, Origin of Life

Numerous legends and stories in various peculiar manners tell of the ancient beginnings of Dubrovnik's emergence, yet among them the most complete is the one that links the making of the city with the Laus Peninsula, a hard cliff that was began to be inhabited by refugees from Epidaurum in the 7th century A.D. The site at the foundations of which emerged today's Cavtat, 16 kilometers East of Dubrovnik, was a Greek-Roman colony in the 7th century. Following the attack of the Slavs and the Mongolian Avars, the frightened residents of Epidaurum -that had been completely devastated by the invaders' attacks-

Cannons defended the city's freedom

escaped towards Laus where they began to make a new settlement on forest landscape and the surrounding inaccessible sharp rocks.

The name Laus comes from the Latin word Lave, Raus, Rausium, Ragussium. Lave is a word of Greek origin, it means cliff, while labes in Latin denotes a steep or a deep abyss. All of these names clarify the look of the island that due to its specific steeps and expressed cliffs turned towards the sea made possible in a certain way also an excellent strategic position for the refugees from Epidaurum. The island had a specific morphology, it was characterized by a look of almost a nature

made fortress that provided the newcomers with ideal protection from the pugnacious invaders.

Nevertheless, the inhabitants who were exhausted from the invaders' attacks began to build defense walls from processed rocks as soon as they arrived to Laus.

Right before the end of the 13th century the settlement obtained its first defense wall made of lime and stone, one that has to some insignificant degree been preserved until today. During the 14th century the settlement spread to also the Eastern part of the island, it is bordered by walls even this day and has kept its name Pustijerna. It had but one entrance, the one from the side of Pile.

The new residents of Laus encountered already existing original inhabitants on the peninsula, and as time passed the settlement spread more and more towards the Northern regions. On the other side of the peninsula a Croatian settlement began to develop simultaneously, one that was in time named Dubrovnik. By strengthening the ties between these two inhabited locations, all the more intensive trade, and the increase in the population, the border between them in time became narrow. The alluvium that filled the borderline between the peninsula and the mainland physically also contributed to the joining of the two sites that became a whole during the 11th century. The joining of the former Laus and the old Croatian settlement occurred at the location of today's Placa or Stradun, which has to this day retained its reputation of the widest and most famous street in Dubrovnik.

Left:
The round Tower
of Minčeta dominates

On the next page:
Placa (Stradun)

The Beginnings of Urban Life

The newly created union gradually began to be filled with a number of structures. The diligent constructors began to build Dubrovnik's great walls as time passed, walls that by the 13th century completely surrounded the Northern section of the city. Since that century the city grew in importance, it became the crossroads of important and quite safe caravan trails that connected the seaside with the interior of the Balkan Peninsula. The secure fortress walls guaranteed Dubrovnik protection from potential invaders, yet in the same time the city began to create its navy, more precisely a strong maritime defense that could resist the attacks of an aggressor.

First records of this old city date back from the year of 1189, they are registered within the documentation of the Bosnian Ban (Vice-Roy, Civil governor) Kulin. These documents permitted the people of Dubrovnik trade privileges, something that speaks volumes of the strength and significance of the city and its citizens.

Byzantine and Venetian Conquering Aspirations

The fortified city that had a well-developed commerce, a rich navy, and was situated at an important crossroads very early on caught the eye of rich and war mongering neighbors to the East and the West. Byzantine and Venice noted the importance of Dubrovnik at a very early stage. To Byzantine the stone city represented a point where for them a very important controlling of the passage of ships along the East Adriatic coast could be performed. The wealthy Venice on the other hand considered Dubrovnik to be a competitor that was growing in strength, and that itself was sufficient enough reason to attempt an invasion.

Rule of Rector

Since the 12th century the city of Dubrovnik was under the rule of a Rector (Knez), who was chosen by the citizens among themselves. Good fruits of the trade labor already in that time lead to a gradual class division of the population, so that higher-class rich clans began to be formed in the city, or the so-called *vlastela* (estate-owners). As it could have been expected, the proprietors gradually began to run the city and hold all more significant political and economic positions. As time passed the city began to transform into an aristocratic republic, and with the strengthening of its borders, ownership, power and wealth, it was becoming all the more lucrative for enemies. This resulted in the attack of the Venetians who in 1205 claimed Dubrovnik as their own.

The Republic of Dubrovnik

Venetian rule ended as late as the year of 1358, when Dubrovnik accepted Hungarian-Croatian rulers. As opposed to the resilient Venetians, the new high command did not meddle with any internal policies of Dubrovnik, which resulted in the creation of an emancipated and independent aristocratic republic. Dubrovnik thus became

The Fortress of St. Ivan oversees
the departure of ships from the old city harbor

a free royal city-state, or, as historical documents describe, the Republic of Dubrovnik.

The unstable political situation in the Mediterranean caused during those unsteady centuries frequent changes in the rule over Dubrovnik. When the Croatian-Hungarian kings lost to the Turks, the people of Dubrovnik had to pay contributions to the new rulers. However, with this they obtained the possibility of making their own interior policies.

The Estate-owners of Dubrovnik (*Vlastela*)

By the 16th century the process of class division of the people of Dubrovnik ended, and it resulted in the existence of three classes.

The wealthiest, the fewest and those with the most power were called *vlastela* (estate-owners), the largest portion of the population belonged to the other class, while the third class consisted of a group of the so-called good citizens who were oftentimes organized in brotherhoods. The good citizens frequently had strong sources of income, were often in regards to wealth equal to the *vlastela*, yet they differed only in the fact that they did not own land.

This kind of social division remained until the fall of the Republic of Dubrovnik, which in turn automatically marked the end of Dubrovnik's political independence. The *vlastela* had, besides land ownership rights, the right to decisions in political issues of the state, and in time its number constantly grew.

Cathedral and rooftops of the old city center

The City Statute determined the direction and width of streets as well as the slope of rooftops

The *Vlastela* (Estate-owners) in Numbers

It has been calculated that during the mid 16th century there were 1500 estate-owners in Dubrovnik, and their grouping into certain oligarchic groups that jointly decided on issues concerning the development of the state was also of importance. Some data indicates that around 1/7 of the population of the Republic of Dubrovnik was part of the *vlastela* in the mid 16th century.

The estate-owners (*vlastela*) also appropriated their right to decision making regarding all strategically important issues onto the male members of their families who were of age, and who within the frame of certain laws of the Republic joined the Great Council of the Republic when they turned 18 years of age. The Great Council was the basis of state rule; the Senate, Small Council and the Rector were all elected from its ranks, as well as all other more important state bodies.

The Senate function was that of true leadership over the Republic, and until the year of 1490 it consisted of 51 senators. Their number increased over time. This kind of a social division in the form of three classes remained until as late as the year of 1808, when the Republic of Dubrovnik fell and independence was lost.

On the other hand, the Small Council had the role of an executive body of the Great Council and Senate rule. The Rector of the Republic of Dubrovnik was elected from these ranks, and his mandate lasted only one month. He governed the activities of each Council, and during his mandate he practically never left his residence, the Rector's Court. The only time he ever left the premises was during necessary state protocol manifestations.

The City's Statute

Dubrovnik was one of the cities that way back in 1272 organized its internal regulations and complete social relations by a city Statute. This legal document regulated by its provisions all of the most important issues, from those political in nature to those that regulated commerce as well as the terms of urbanism. The leadership decision reached in 1278 illustrates the correctly and exactly drafted city organization and the correctly verified provisions, a decision that stipulated a long term storage and strict safeguard of documents, books, materials in archives and adopted legal documents concerning the functioning and activities of the entire community.

This decision that provided future generations with inexhaustible city materials remained in full force until the year of 1808, so until the fall of the Republic of Dubrovnik, and it resulted in historical materials of exquisite value that are to this day being kept in the Historical Archives of Dubrovnik.

Expansion of Commerce

Dubrovnik shall in history also stay known as the Republic that paid special attention to the development of its economy. Despite the fact that Venice when it reigned attempted to minimize its commercial significance, skilled traders of Dubrovnik expanded their business far and wide. The exceptional fleet of ships -another acquisition of Dubrovnik- helped them in this; it made possible to these crafty traders exceptionally broad market directions. As opposed to Venice, Byzantine leadership had much softer opinions regarding the commercial expansions of Dubrovnik, by all means, it in no way hindered the ever increasing manufacturing productivity of the city, nor the development of maritime affairs. Byzantine even made it possible for Dubrovnik to create strong connections and privileged relations throughout the empire, which resulted in a number of charters of friendship and business-trade contracts that the crafty people of Dubrovnik drafted with their new partners.

People of Dubrovnik - Skilled Traders

As skilled traders, the people of Dubrovnik filled caravans with large quantities of salted fish, salt, textile fabric and pottery, and in return they obtained ore, livestock and various raw materials.

In times of the Republic of Dubrovnik, the strongest branch of commerce was based on the production and transport of ore, silver, lead, potassium and copper, as well as other materials from Bosnian and Serbian mines, which were introduced to the insatiable market of Europe.

The traders of Dubrovnik acquired a great amount of wealth by means of this very branch of commerce, and this wealth also reflected in the renting of a number of mines that provided their owners from the Republic of Dubrovnik with great profits on a daily basis. In addition to Europe, the valuable ore was also transported by ships to Venice, France and Spain.

The production of textile fabric was also very developed in those days. By trading ore for materials, businessmen from Dubrovnik obtained Catalonian wool from Italy and Spain, wool that they processed in spinning-mills, workshops and dye-houses in Rijeka and Župa of Dubrovnik. Fabric of very high quality was then transported and sold on the current European market. The able people who processed fabric also began importing silk from Levant, which they also offered to the European market following processing.

Steep streets and stairways with numerous shops represent a typical picture of Dubrovnik

This part of production was shut down during the Turkish invasions, which severed some commerce routes, and the disabling of these activities also occurred due to the devastation of workshops that were located outside the protective walls of Dubrovnik.

Shipbuilding Force

As early as the ninth century Dubrovnik could take pride in its respectable navy that progressively grew during the century, and it reached full blossom in the period of the Republic of Dubrovnik.

The fact that supports this claim is that Dubrovnik during the mid 16th century had around 180 sailing ships and a crew that numbered more than five thousand seamen. Maritime affairs were exceptionally developed in Dubrovnik, and it is deemed that during the golden age of its development almost one of eight citizens of the Republic had a

true connection with the far seas. It was exactly the maritime affairs and shipbuilding along with commerce that provided Dubrovnik with the largest amount of income. Innovations that the people of Dubrovnik used to incorporate into their exceptionally developed shipbuilding industry can best be described by the notion of shipbuilding -the Dubrovnik way. This Dubrovnik way represented construction of ships with clear and simple design lines.

With its 180 ships that had a total bearing capacity of 36 thousand wagons and the total value of around 700 thousand gold coins, Dubrovnik earned the epithet of a first-class shipbuilding force during the 70-ies in the 16th century. The ships of Dubrovnik sailed throughout the Mediterranean, all the way up to England, and not even routes that lead to Africa and India were unfamiliar to them.

The diversity of the vessels was impressive as well, in addition to sailing ships, the Dubrovnik seamen also had navas (large ships), small rowing vessels (šajke), trabacolas, galleys, galleons, caravels,

The Bokar Fort and the impressive Lovrijenac Fortress

carracks, and frigates, which were all exceptionally equipped -navigation wise. All these top-notch vessels were built in domestic construction yards located in Gruž, Slani, Lopud, Brsečine and on Šipan, and their quality was evidence of the knowledge and excellence of Dubrovnik's caulkers.

In addition to specific Dubrovnik construction, these ships were also known for the unique manner of their initial lowering into the sea, sideways, which was at that time a very modern shipbuilding innovation.

Other than shipbuilding, Dubrovnik was also strong in diplomatic connections. At the end of the 18th century the city had a number of consulates in more than 80 cities.

Another interesting piece of information was that in that time Dubrovnik had truly the greatest blossoming in ship capital, there were more than 650 sailing ships and fishing boats that sailed the seas, of which 200 even sailed on ocean waters.

St. Vlaho

The city's guard and protector, advocate of heaven and savior hides under the name of Saint Vlaho. The people of Dubrovnik chose him as saint protector in the year of 971, which is a consequence of a story that speaks of one of the numerous Venetian siege attempts. During this siege, St. Vlaho -who is a martyr and a bishop- saved the city. Ever since then St. Vlaho has been the true protector of the city, and the people of Dubrovnik honor him every year on the 3rd of February since 1190, by means of a traditional city wide celebration.

The City's Heritage

Dubrovnik entered the Middle Ages with two-thirds of today's city core, defined buildings, stonemason's ornaments, and also numerous new sacral structures that followed the ever-increasing needs of the population.

In the 14th century the city entirely covered the space within the walls. The walls have taken on a formed shape, at some locations additions were made to them, on the side towards the mainland and the harbor 15 square forts were added, and streets within the city were clearly defined. Parallel to the shape of the wall, a number of new structures were being built within the city itself; the construction of the cathedral had been completed by then, and next to the gates from the East and West sides of the city construction of the Dominican and the Franciscan monasteries began.

Dubrovnik had a pharmacy located inside the Franciscan monastery as early as 1317, a fact that speaks volumes about the rich history of the city and the level of cultural awareness. This is the oldest pharmacy in Europe, and it still actively does business in the Franciscan monastery.

Dubrovnik also retained a hospital from its days of advance blossom, one that was founded in the 14th century, as well as the first

Right:
St. Vlaho observes the sea
from Southern city walls

quarantine in the world -founded in the year of 1377. This quarantine was built, among other things, for the prevention of potential diseases that the city's citizens, meaning seamen, could spread among the other citizens.

The city stood out from primitive principles by many characteristics, and by the contents it possessed it kept pace with other European urban centers. For example, instead of wooden ones, houses made of stone that mostly included a ground floor, two floors and an attic space appeared more and more frequently. Waste was thrown out from the back side of the building into a sewer line, which was connected into the one still active today as part of the city's sewer system.

In addition to the pharmacy and the hospital, the developed culture and fine arts, the city in 1624 obtained a high education institution Collegium Ragusinum, that was founded by the Jesuitical Order, and that was by special decree 30 years later promoted into Public Academy for Arts and Science.

The Jewish Community

Open to new experiences and cultures, during the 14th, 15th and 16th century Dubrovnik accepted a small group of Jews, mostly traders. They found a new location for life after escaping from Spanish-Portuguese regions. In addition to commerce, the Jewish community over generations provided highly educated citizens -mostly doctors. The Jews lived in their own part of the city, a ghetto of a sort, yet they had a quite liberal co-existence. They did not enjoy citizen status; they were treated as community members headed by consuls.

Regardless, the Jewish community enjoyed certain privileges, so as opposed to people of different religions they did not have to leave the section of the city that is fortified by walls at the sound of the evening bell. Jews mostly inhabited the region of today's Lahaska and Judoka Streets, and they had their synagogue that was built in 1408.

The curious fact regarding this synagogue -that emerged by means of an adaptation of a residential structure- is that even today it serves the same purpose, and considering how old it is and its continuous existence, it is right behind the one in Prague.

Left:
Stradun - the city's jugular

Substantial Cultural Heritage

The absence of exhausting wars that would have impoverished the huge budget of the city, as well as the investment of funds into culture and science resulted in the fact that Dubrovnik was successful in enriching its future generations with a heritage of a number of representative works from all areas of art and science. As early as the 15th century Dubrovnik could boast of its big poets, and among them a special place was taken by Karlo Pucić and the famous Ilija Cirević.

The names of Džora Držić and Šiško Menčetić must be mentioned regarding renaissance poets, but the famous Marin Držić and Ivan Gundulić, the poet author of the poem Osman, deserved to be on a special page in the history of Dubrovnik.

Famous and inspired thinkers also hailed from Dubrovnik throughout history, such as Benko Kotruljić, Nikola Sagrojević, mathematician, physicist and optician Marin Getaldić. The head of that list is definitely physicist and mathematician Ruđer Bošković.

Great Earthquake

What wars and ruthless invasions by competitors had not succeeded in taking care of was done so by the catastrophic earthquake that occurred on the 6th of April 1667. Great trembles of the ground that also happened in 1520 and in 1637 dared to touch into the foundations of Dubrovnik's economy, but this catastrophic one in 1667 completely wiped out the entire life of the wealthy city.

Following the earthquake a great fire ravaged through the city, and during these several horrific days, by some estimations around five thousand people lost their lives in Dubrovnik, while only two to three thousand managed to survive.

The catastrophic quake destroyed numerous beautiful buildings, palaces; it devastated the old Romanic cathedral, monasteries and churches, and took into oblivion numerous documents, files and legal documents that had recorded each historical detail of the city. The famous fleet of ships of Dubrovnik that was at that moment docked in the city harbor was also destroyed.

Monument of poet Ivan Gundulić,
located on a higher-up section of the square

Fascinating façade of the Sponza Palace

The damage was all too large, and Dubrovnik suffered to recover from it. Numerous persons who hailed from Dubrovnik yet were residing elsewhere throughout the world held out a helping hand, and did not spare expenses in order to return the city to its normal state.

New style of construction encompassed shapes of Roman baroque, and the old special and picturesque style of construction that was used in the city prior to the catastrophic earthquake was in part abandoned, Only the Sponza Palace and parts of the Rector's Court façade sur-

*Gate of Buže, one of the
stone gates to the city*

vived the quake and remained in its original shape and form.

A large portion of the Vlastela (estate-owners) also lost their lives during the great earthquake, so for the first time members of the five most distinguished families in the city became part of the Great Council. A great number of devastated buildings forced the city's leadership to consider leaving the city for good, but reason and strength prevailed. Dubrovnik once again began to rise upon the ruins of old beauty, and with it also new buildings that remain to this day. Unfortunately, as a consequence of the earthquake the city began to slowly lose the primate it had in its most famous times. The crash in a certain way denoted also the beginning of the end. Tremulous times followed during the end of the 18th century and the beginning of the 19th, ones that lead to the city losing its autonomy. Dubrovnik had to lose its long preserved freedom. This, on the other hand, was not due to the earthquake; it was due to the legendary general Napoleon, who in 1808 ended the independence of the Republic of Dubrovnik. Although some believed that with the fall of this great warrior the mighty Republic of Dubrovnik would rise again, it all remained just hope. The Austrian empire decisively and strongly opposed these desires; it cleverly used the weak state of the city and placed it under its rule.

However, history recorded the significance of this liberal and cultural city, which UNESCO included into its list of the world's cultural heritage on account of the architecture of its historical core in 1979. Does that not say a lot about all the glamour of the stone lace of this Mediterranean beauty?

*Left:
The St. Ivan Fortress*

A STROLL THROUGH THE CITY

The center of the city was before and still remains the Placa, or more popularly called Stradun, a place that in Dubrovnik's history used to be the connecting point between the inhabitants of the Laus peninsula and the Croatian community that was situated on the other side of the channel. The Placa is the heart of the city around which streets and alleys spread like fish bones, entirely filled with beautiful structures.

The city's leadership had from the very beginning planned in detail all elements of proper construction, locating the key architectural buildings at the edges of Stradun with almost exact precision.

Stone beauty and harmony of Stradun

The great earthquake that had destroyed a considerable number of structures and the fire that followed forced the leaders to establish a new way of construction within urbanistic plans. Thus, the houses on Stradun were no longer wooden, they were exclusively made of stone, and lined up in two rows they entirely resembled each other with their facades and shape. The new physical planners had a strict eye for order and form, presenting among other things a great dose of wisdom and skill. A number of laws by the city administration also disabled construction of wooden houses within city walls because they presented a constant threat to life and the safety of the city and its citizens due to frequent fires.

Facades of Stradun

Everything was under strict control. The law - more precisely the city's Statute - did not only determine stone as the sole construction material. It also determined the direction and width of streets, the slope of rooftops, the size of windows and thresholds as well as of other elements. This resulted in a number of very similar houses that had business premises on the ground floor as ornaments.

This form has been kept successfully until this very day. Stradun is a square of stone, the road that people of Dubrovnik and numerous

guests walk every day, impressed by the simple elegance of living art. Stradun is deeply rooted into all pores of city life, filled with numerous cafés and shops. Clean and orderly, bathed in sunrays and filled with a great amount of light, it is an unavoidable vein of the city where life takes place. Everything that happens in the city happens on Stradun. Ceremonies and celebrations start from there, stories begin to spread from there. Stradun is in addition to being the jugular of the city also the true brave heart of the old city.

City Walls

The walls always attract attention, and if one takes into consideration that the defense side walls of Dubrovnik are one of the most beautiful and best preserved middle age fortifications, it is no wonder that there are so many tourists who wish to rummage through their past. The walls provide Dubrovnik with a specific look, they spread 1940 meters without cutoffs, and they consist of a system of bastions, forts, old Turkish-style jails, towers and separate fortresses.

They were the inexhaustible work of ingenious construction workers, but also of clear heads of the leaders of Dubrovnik who by crowning the city with strong fortifications obtained primarily the security

Dubrovnik - a bird's eye perspective

of the soft inner core. Walls surrounded the city as early as the 13th century, with the exception of the Dominican monastery, and a century later that religious structure was also included in the contents of the firm stone belt.

Nothing was left to chance. The walls were constantly renewed and updated in time. In order to even better safeguard the city core from potential invader attacks, in the 14th century they were strengthened by 15 square towers.

The walls were made in accordance to an exactly detailed plan. At some places their height is 25 meters, and they also differ in thickness.

In sections facing the sea, for example, their thickness varies from one to three meters, while sections facing land amount to up to five meters. Additional lower slanted foundations reinforce some sections of the wall facing the sea. The walls are surrounded by three round and 14 square towers, two corner forts, five bastions and one fortress. The slightly irregular look of stone bricks at the corners was remedied by strong forts; the mighty self-supported fortress Lovrijenac is situated on the West, the round tower Minčeta is on the North side, fortress Revelin defends the city harbor on the East, while St. Ivan guards the Southeastern side of the city.

In the old days it was possible to enter the city through four entrances. One gate called Ploče was in the East, the Pile Gate was located in the West, while two gates, the Gate of Ponte (the harbor) and the fish market gate lead into the harbor. The gates into the city did not directly make possible contact with the city core; there were a few more gates and several passages that guaranteed ideal security for citizens.

The City Harbor was very well protected as well, it had a great break-water structure Kaše that protected it from strong winds.

The walls were a mighty protection from invaders, yet deep moats and more than 130 cannons that were made in domestic manufacturing plants also contributed to this protection.

Lovrijenac

"Non bene pro toto libertas venditur auro", Freedom is not to be sold even for all the gold in the world, states the sign at the entrance of Lovrijenac.

This monumental, self-supported fortress that was raised upon a rock that is 37 meters high, is the true protector from invader attacks, as well as a mighty structure that leaves visitors breathless with its greatness. Its existence has been known since the 14th century, although some data indicates that its construction began during the 11th century. It has experienced numerous renovations during time, but it has definitely kept its specific triangular shaped form that adheres to the shape of the rocks upon which it was made even in design plans. It is characterized also by the specific structural form -the longest surface faces towards Bokar, which makes it that Lovrijenac stands as a shield over Kalarinja, a small harbor of Dubrovnik.

In its history Lovrijenac had 10 large cannons, and the largest and most famous one named "Gušter" (Lizard) was designed by Ivan Rabljanin. In its interior, Lovrijenac had a square court yard, and it is also interesting due to the fact that it had walls facing the outside that are 12 meters thick for security reasons. The other section facing the Western city walls does not exceed 60 centimeters in thickness.

Lovrijenac is often called the Gibraltar of Dubrovnik, and that nickname was also given because of its protective role. Numerous

The impressive Lovrijenac Fortress was erected upon a 37-meter high cliff

legends that clarify the motives for its construction follow the fortress that two mobile bridges lead to, and one of them claims that in the 11th century Venice had decided to build a spectacular fort on that location, with the help of which it could keep the entire Dubrovnik under

its rule as if on a palm of the hand -long term. Be that as it may, the wise people of Dubrovnik discovered this wicked plan, and decided to construct a mighty defense fortification as soon as possible. The story goes on to say that it took them three months in total to build the Lovrijenac Fortress. The finished fortification on the top of the hill, legend states, greatly surprised the Venetian ships that were full of material for the construction of their never built fort, so they very quickly turned back towards the West.

During the centuries that ensued the purpose of Lovrijenac varied, and in the recent times it mostly serves as one of the most beautiful stages in the world for Shakespeare's Hamlet.

The Minčeta Tower

It is the work of Dubrovnik's constructor Nicifor Ranjina, who began to build this structure in the 14th century. It provides the best view of Dubrovnik. This is one of the most important defense points of Dubrovnik, built upon the former estate of the Mančetić family, due to which it was named Minčeta.

It is a wonderful tower, the highest point of the walls of Dubrovnik. It is characteristic by its built in embrasures for guns, it is one of the symbols of Dubrovnik, as well as one of the most beautiful forts in the world.

Ranjina, the constructor, began to build Minčeta in the year of 1319. His initial plan was to build a strong square tower, but turbulent events that threatened with new attacks and the plague forced the people of Dubrovnik to design an additional construction project. They employed Michelozzo di Bartolomeo of Florence to be the author of updating the existing fortifications.

He skillfully built a wide fortification around the existing tower of Minčeta, one whose walls were six meters thick and had in them a number of openings for cannons.

After Michelozzo, a sculptor virtuoso from Zadar Juraj Dalmatinac undertook work on the impressive tower of Minčeta, who built a round tower. Its construction was finally finished in 1464. There is a massive crown on top of Minčeta that has more of an aesthetic role than a protective one. The gatehouse of this fortress had three floors of halls with Turkish-style jails, embrasures for guns and openings for cannons. The fortress was in historical times armed with nine cannons, and among them was a bronze work of Ivan Rabljanin. During the time of Austrian occupation the work was cut apart and transported to Vienna.

The Minčeta Tower,
one of the most beautiful forts in the world

The Revelin Fortress

This is yet another impressive palace, a true stone protector of the East side of the city. Revelin was built in the 16th century, outside of city walls, and its task was to guard the mainland approach on the East side of the city and to provide a good look upon the Gate of Ploče, the East entrance to the stone city center.

Its name comes from the word rivelino, which denotes a specific kind of a defense structure that is built on a location situated opposite to the entrance into the city's gate.

The fortress was being built a full 11 years, and the project was designed and executed by Antonio Ferramolino.

All other bigger construction and reconstruction jobs in the city were halted while the Revelin was being built. The city's leadership wanted to increase security on the East side of the city at any cost, and while a little frightened by the ever growing pretensions of Venice they ventured into the project without regard to neither the manpower nor the means.

One part of Revelin is a steep drop down to the sea, and protection was in those turbulent historical times guaranteed by moats that surrounded it on its three other sides. The interior provided sufficient space, so assemblies of the Great Council were held in it. Today Revelin is used during the period of the Dubrovnik Summer Festival as an ideal theatre stage.

Right:
The Ploče Gate and the Revelin Fortress,
protector of the East side of the city

The St. Ivan Fortress

Yet another monumental fortress, and in addition a flawless defense point of the city. The St. Ivan Fortress was conceived as the main point for the defense of the city's harbor, and soon it became one of the most important positions in the city's fortifications.

Initial construction on this fortress, often also called the Mulo tower, began way back in the 14th century. In time it had been added on to and renovated, but in the 16th century it obtained its final look. During the 14th century the fortress got its first tower, but during the ensuing two years much was added to it, so it had its final shape in the 16th century. The author that is being connected to its existence is constructor Paskoje Miličević from Dubrovnik. The side of St. Ivan fortress that faces the sea consists of rounded and slightly inclined walls, while towards the harbor it is ornamented by tough and straight

rocks that provide additional required security. The St. Ivan Fortress is a very interesting structure that along with the St. Luka Tower, situated on the opposite side of the old City Harbor, constitutes a mutual wholeness.

Miličević was well meritorious for the construction of this entire protection complex of Dubrovnik, and among other things he also left his signature upon the construction project of Dubrovnik's Kaše harbor break-water.

There is a Maritime Museum that safeguards a collection of valuable documents, paintings and objects from Dubrovnik's past located within the St. Ivan Fortress. Also in the fortress one can find the well-known Aquarium that consists of 27 aquariums that present the great wealth of fauna.

The Fortress of St. Ivan guards the entrance to the old city harbor

Forts of Mrtvo zvono and Bokar

Monumental fortifications of Dubrovnik offer joy that long remains in memory. They are also interesting for they create an entire system of mutually connected defense points, and each of them provides a fantastic view upon the city and the wide sea. From the St. Ivan fortress towards Lovrijenac also lays the fort of Mrtvo Zvono, whose initial construction dates back to the 16th century. Paskoje Miličević, the already famous constructor, was responsible for its construction as well. He designed this yet another defensive fortification, and it also had a number of openings for cannons. Next in order on the way from fort Mrtvo zvono towards Lovrijenac comes the fort of Bokar, or in transla-

The Bokar Fortress is used as a stage for the Dubrovnik Summer Festival

tion Zvjezdan (of a star), which is the work of the Florence man Michellozo. It was built in the year of 1461, and its task was the defense of the Pile Gate and protection of the mainland approach to Dubrovnik.

The Bokar fort has a specific cylindrical shape, and it is partly built upon a sea cliff. It unifies within itself the impressive channels with the sea. It was built exclusively for defense from mainland attacks, and within it had storage rooms in which weapons and ammunition were kept during unstable periods. Due to its unique monumental look and quality it is today also used as an excellent theater stage for the Dubrovnik Summer Festival.

The Pile Gate

Along with the Ploče gate that is located in the East section of the city, the Pile Gate -located on the West side of Dubrovnik - represents one of the two most important entry points for passage into the narrow city center. During history the city only had four gates; two on the mainland side and two from the harbor. Stone bridges that had wooden mobile bridges at the outer gates lead to the gate on the mainland side.

The Pile Gate consists of an outer and an inner gate. These were finally realized in 1537, when they obtained their half-circle tower at the outer gate with a statue of St. Vlaho. A mobile bridge that was raised each evening followed by a special ceremony after which this entrance to the city was closed gave the gate a special characteristic.

The bridge had under it a deep moat that also played a defensive role.

Along with the statue of St. Vlaho, there are also three stone head sculptures over the main gate that portray one bearded man and two women. Although the true meaning of this stone decoration is unknown, it is assumed that they tell a tale of unhappy love and seductions.

The Pile Gate, situated on the West side of the city, represents one of the most important gates into the old city center

There used to be a square shaped fortress at the location of the current pedestrian serpentine between the gates of Pile. According to data from chronicles it was built in the year of 972. However, as the Austrian occupation began in 1818, the fortress was torn down due to a construction of a road that enabled the only entrance to the city. The fortress was built in 972 for the purpose of a bridgehead, and its interior was used to store wheat.

The Ploče Gate

The Ploče Gate is situated opposite to Pile, on the easternmost side of the city, and it is framed into a strong complex of fortresses, towers and walls. Exactly opposite to this gate is the Revelin fortress, the greatness of which safeguards the East approach to the city. This gate has a stone bridge and a moat as well. The moat was built in the 15th century. This gate is also called the St. Luka Gate, and it consists of an outer and an inner entrance.

A stone bridge that leads to Revelin is located in front of the outer entrance.

Ploče, Eastern gate to the city

The Great Fountain of Onofrio

In the middle of a small square located right next to the Franciscan monastery and the Pile Gate stands the great Fountain of Onofrio, another frequent theme on postcards of Dubrovnik. As opposed to the other Dalmatian cities that supplied themselves with water from large reservoirs where rainwater was kept, the people of Dubrovnik desired to have fresh spring water. It was for this very reason that a decision was made (in 1438) to build a well, the creation of which was entrusted to a constructor from Naples named Onofrio della Cavi. Onofrio thus began to build an aqua duct that brought

Bird's eye perspective of the Great Fountain of Onofrio

water into the city from a spring named Šumet out of the Rijeka Dubrovačka that is 12 kilometers away from Dubrovnik. Onofrio was a true visionary and virtuoso. At the location above Konavle he very lucidly built two separate aqua duct spur-lines, one of which transported water to the Pile region and the other supplied the city. In addition to the great one, the constructor of one of the traits of Dubrovnik also had the Small fountain built, located on the completely opposite side of the city -the lower section of Stradun. Its task was supplying water to the city market on the Luža Square .

The Great Fountain of Onofrio is round, and in addition to supplying drinking water it also serves as a reservoir. The great earthquake nicked also the fountain's architectural beauty, taking into oblivion its former ornaments. Only 16 maskeroni remained behind for future generations, these are figures, and running water comes out of their mouths. The Great Onofrio is a favorite meeting place of young people of Dubrovnik. A curiosity regarding this fountain is that along with the Small Onofrio Fountain it served as a setting in a famous work of Marin Držić -the renaissance comedy Novela od Stanca.

The Luža Square and Orlando's Column

The square is located at the lower part of Stradun. It is in actuality more of an Eastern extension of Placa, and its center is decorated by Orlando's Column, significant among other things because traditional manifestations of Dubrovnik are held upon it. The square is yet another characteristic of Dubrovnik, and another reason for this is the fact that a number of cultural heritage artifacts are situated upon it. Along the Orlando, here as well is the Small Fountain of Onofrio, the Sponza Palace, the Church of St. Vlaho; the Rector's Court is nearby, and also very interesting is the Great Council Palace, the main guardsmen building, the city Bell tower and the Bell tower of Luža.

Orlando's Column is one of the symbols of Dubrovnik's independence and defiance; it is the central part of the Luža Square , located between the Sponza Palace and the church of St. Vlaho. On the column is a likeness of a medieval knight Orlando, after whom it was named. It was built in the 15th century by the sculptor Bonino from Milan, dedicated to the famous knight Orlando who, as legend has it, heroically saved the city from a pirate attack. However, the chronicles are persistent and state that the city raised the statue in honor and glory of King Žigmund, Hungarian-Croatian and Czech king, the protector of Dubrovnik in battles against Venetians. Ever since it was built, up until Napoleon's victory and abolishment of the Republic of Dubrovnik, the flag of the Republic with a likeness of St. Vlaho proudly hung on top of it. In more recent times a flag hangs from the column top during great festivals of Dubrovnik; one dedicated to its protector St. Vlaho and the Dubrovnik Summer Festival.

Orlando's Column otherwise also serves as an ancient measure in the city of Dubrovnik. The length of the elbow on the right arm of Orlando was taken as a measure for length. This is the so-called Dubrovnik elbow whose length amounts to 51.2 centimeters.

The Luža Square, City Bell tower and the Sponza Palace

The Small Fountain of Onofrio

It has already been mentioned that Onofrio della Cava, the author of the Great Fountain, built it as well. Its purpose was to supply the market on Luža with water. During the middle ages only Christians were allowed to use it.

The City Bell tower and the Old Bell tower

These are yet another trademark of the city. The city's bell tower, as a link in a chain rounds off the architectural collection on the Luža Square , one of the most frequently visited city points.

The bell tower is 31 meters high, domestic constructors constructed it, and before it was built the city clock that now decorates it was located on the walls of Rector's Court. Next to the bell tower is a small niche that hides a Small Fountain, the work of sculptor Petar Martinov.

The Old bell tower or otherwise called Luža is located in an attractive area between the City Bell tower and the Sponza Palace. It contained bells used to call for Council assemblies, which were after an explosion of gunpowder at the Rector's Court transported from it to Luža.

The Rector's Court

The Rector's Court is a fascinating palace where the Rector (Knez) used to reside. In addition to being his work area and private residence, this building also served as the headquarters of the Small Council. The Rector's Court is filled with the city's history, it used to contain the armory, gun powder storage room, and lodgings for guards as well as the prison, yet its greatest

significance was the fact that the Rector resided in it during his one month long mandate. The Knez was only allowed to leave the general area of the Court during ceremonial festivities, otherwise each evening he was given the key to the city that he returned early each morning.

Rector's Court, gothic-renaissance palace, 15th century

The Court is a fantastic architectural wholeness that reflects a number of renaissance characteristics intertwined with certain gothic elements. Thus, for example, the ground floor of the building is modeled in renaissance style, the first floor is mostly gothic, and the following ones are yet again filled with pure renaissance style architecture.

The Rector's Court is a spectacular structure and one of the architectural pearls of the rich heritage of Dubrovnik. According to many it is the most beautiful residential palace on the Croatian coast. Throughout history it has been reconstructed and remodeled numerous times, and one of the reasons for this is fires that scorched its spectacular beauty, earthquakes, yet also damage caused by various explosions.

The Court was shaken by a great explosion of its gunpowder room, after which its reconstruction began. This part of the job was initially entrusted to Onofrio di Giordano della Cava, the expert whose name frequently came up concerning historical objects and monuments of Dubrovnik.

Along with the worthy Naples man, Michelozzo di Bartolomeo Michellozzi of Florence and some domestic experts also later on impressed a soul into the Rector's Court by means of their sculpting skills.

Valuable entablatures on the facade of the palace constitute one characteristic of the Rector's Court, upon which are symbolic sculptures that were carved by artist Petar Martinov.

Atrium of the Rector's Court

In addition to an amazing atrium, the place that with its great ambiance serves also as a beautiful stage of stone for numerous concerts and shows, interesting entablatures on the facade of the Rector's Court also attract attention, as well as the bell that is located on the

Valuable capitels the façade of the palace characterize the Rector's Court

first floor and the sculpture of Miho Pracat, an honored citizen. Besides the fact that it represents an architectural and historically valuable structure of Dubrovnik, the Rector's Court is today a building of the Historical Department of the Museum of Dubrovnik as well.

The Sponza Palace

Just like the Rector's Court, the Sponza Palace also represents an architectural union of several various styles - renaissance to gothic. This is definitely one of the most beautiful palaces in the city, located to the left of Luža. It is today the headquarters of the Historical Archives; it is the work of expert Paskoje Miličević and the Andrijić brothers. Today the palace contains the headquarters of the Historical Archives, but it used to be a customs center, that was why it had been called Divona (in Italian dogana means customs). The palace is of a rectangular shape. It contains a courtyard in the interior, and towards the square it has a beautiful porch that also exists on the first courtyard floor.

In addition to its exceptional beauty and historical value, the Sponza Palace also has a significance regarding the treasure that is being kept in it. This treasure is a large number of documents that tell a vivid tale about the history of this city and its principles of freedom, and there exist around seven thousand volumes of manuscripts and around one hundred thousand particular individual manuscripts. The Historical Archive also guards the Statute of Dubrovnik and a number of documents from the famous Republic of Dubrovnik.

The luxurious Sponza Palace,
16th century

The Gundulić Field

With its special color and life that puts a seal on everyday life, The Gundulić Field represents yet another hot spot of the city. In its center is a monument of the famous artist of Dubrovnik, poet Ivan Gundulić, erected in 1892. The monumental statue -work of Ivan Rendić- is located on a raised section of the square that is often used as an impressive drama stage during summers. The base of the statue also bears inscriptions from Gundulić's work Osman, his best-known epic poem.

Lazaret and Arsenal of Dubrovnik

Another significant structure established in the 17th century and located outside city walls in the region of Ploče. Lazaret always had the role of a health center, almost an isolated hotel in which seamen were kept in quarantine after returning from the far seas.

Lazaret was yet another proof of the health enlightenment of the people of Dubrovnik and their care for preserving and maintaining the quality of life.

The complex of Lazaret is divided into two parts, it has a ground floor consisting of five separate rooms, and the upper floor was conceived in the same way. This role of the upper floor remained until the 19th century.

Near Lazaret there is also one of the most popular beaches of Dubrovnik named Banje (Banja translated means bathroom). Strollers through the city do not avoid Arsenal either, a row of four overhead covered spaces, located in the City Harbor. War ships used to be built in it, and its role was to guard the galleys that defended the city. Today Arsenal serves for the accommodation of the famous City Coffee-House that provides a view towards the attractive City Harbor.

The great Arsenal had four storage spaces for galleys. In 1345 it was closed for purposes of better defense of the city, and in 1386 the construction of outer arches began that had afterwards been expanded several times. The Arsenal was later extended eastward, and pursuant to the decision in 1494, the extended arches had to be walled shut every time after they were used. In this way the tradition of galley construction was preserved.

Left:
Under the arches of Sponza Palace

DUBROVNIK'S SACRAL HERITAGE RICHES

A wide range of beautiful structures of sacral heritage is one of the characteristic traits of Dubrovnik. A more widespread occurrence of sacral structures in the city was recorded as early as the ninth century, and through the following two decades there had been an exceptional influence of pre-Romanic elements. The manner of construction supports this statement. It is based on the existence of smaller single-storey structures with three beams, the unavoidable half-circle arch, and a dome. As commerce and contacts with other countries developed, the city turned all the more to new artistic notions -thus since the 11th century Romanic influence is notable. It just may be that such artistic guidelines would have mostly been promoted by the Church of St. Vlaho -at least judging by one description dating from

Rector's Court and the Cathedral of Dubrovnik

the year of 1440- if the great earthquake had not leveled it. The earthquake, but also fires that swallowed a range of the luxurious architecture were not however able to take into oblivion the Benedictine monastery, the church on Lokrum and one other example of unbelievably beautiful architecture - the monastery church on a small lake island on Mljet.

As time passed the city obtained prettier sights, and also nice monuments that were pleasing to the eye. In addition to the Franciscan and the Dominican monasteries, the city can also boast of a number of other structures whose architecture is wonderful, which on the inside offer a number of valuable works of art and details that represent a way of life from some distant time.

Church of St. Vlaho

If any one church bears the seal of Dubrovnik, then it is St. Vlaho's - the dominant structure located on lower Stradun. The gothic church dedicated to the protector of Dubrovnik St. Vlaho was built by Marino Gropelli, an Italian, and he created his demanding project at the location of the old Romanic church that was devastated in the great earthquake. A detailed wide stairway, a large ornamented portal and an oval dome in the middle shape the impressive sacral structure situated across from the Sponza Palace. Its interior is carefully decorated;

Procession on the holiday of St. Vlaho

special attention was paid to a number of details. For example, it has luxurious altars, and the main one contains a statue of St. Vlaho made of gold-plated silver from the 15th century.

The statue holds in its hands a scale model of the city, showing exactly what Dubrovnik looked like prior to the great and devastating earthquake. Although the church had not, the statue survived the earthquake, which lead the people into believing in the miracle of the statue.

The Cathedral of Dubrovnik

Similar to the Church of St. Vlaho, this yet another sacral structure also stood at the location where the old Romanic cathedral was prior to the great earthquake. The full name of the new cathedral is Dubrovnik's Main Church of Mary's Assumption, it was built in the 18th century, and Stjepan Gradić -a famous intellectual of Dubrovnik, who held the position of head of the Vatican library, especially supported its construction. The project was entrusted to constructor Andreo Buffalini, who designed the church in great detail filled with elements of baroque.

Construction of the church began in 1671 by constructor Paolo Andreotti. The Cathedral of Dubrovnik is characteristic by its facade that rises upwards in seven ledge-stairs, and inside it is worth seeing a few late baroque period altars. The church used to have a rich treasury that lost a great deal of its artifacts during the great earthquake, and among the more valuable ones were artifacts of the head and hands of Saint Vlaho. The treasury also contains a number of valuable paintings, for example the Romanic-Byzantine icon of Our Lady with the Child and the Great multi-part painting of Mary's Assumption that was made in the workshop of Tizian.

A story about the former Romanic church that preceded today's sacral monument constitutes another curiosity concerning the establishment of the Cathedral of Dubrovnik. Legend states that king Richard the Lionhearted helped build the former Romanic church after finding salvation from a shipwreck by Lokrum Island in 1192.

Several historical altars are kept within the Cathedral of Dubrovnik,
one of them being the one for St. Ivan Nepomuk

The famous garden and closed courtyard of the Franciscan monastery

Franciscan Monastery

Erected in the 14th century by domestic authors Mihoje Brajkov and Leonardo and Petar Petrović, the monastery represented all the luxury and imagination of Dubrovnik's construction. Two closed courtyards harmonize the shape of the monastery. The larger one is Romanic in style, slightly intermixed with elements of pure gothic style. This clash can best be noted in the reduction of interior court-yards to a row of characteristic arcades. The closed courtyard is the work of sculptor Brajkov, while brothers were responsible for the main church portal that bears the depiction of crying over the dead Christ.

The great complex of the Franciscan monastery is situated at the West entrance to Placa, right next to the Gate of Pile. Spatially it extends northbound all the way to Minčeta. During the first phase of its establishment it was outside city walls, but due to constant invasion attempts it was placed within the fortifications system. The complex entails a range of elements; the remains of the old Franciscan church

are at this location, which was leveled by the earthquake. Today's church built in baroque style was erected in its former spot. The closed interior courtyard of the church attracts special attention, it is by many accounts one of the most beautiful ones in Dubrovnik.

Another unique quality of the Franciscan monastery is its pharmacy, the third oldest one in the world. Ever since the year of 1317 it has continually been active within this impressive architectural structure, and it remains so to this day. The monastery pharmacy attracts attention with the beauty of its old bottles and flasks, however, the ancient wealth of this institution lies in the library that is deemed to be one of the most famous ones in the world.

The Franciscans of Dubrovnik guard a collection that numbers more than 20 thousand pieces of literature, and among them are around 1200 old manuscripts of invaluable cultural and historical value, 137 incunabula (old medieval books, first print examples) and seven old church books.

Closed interior courtyard of the Franciscan monastery, impressive work of sculptor Brajkov

Up:
The Franciscan monastery pharmacy is one
of the oldest and best preserved in Europe

Up (left and right):
Colonnade ornaments depict grotesque
characters and mythical creatures

Right:
Portal of the Franciscan church

Dominican monastery

The Dominican monastery complex is located in the East section of the city, opposite to the Franciscan monastery. Chronicles mention the Dominican monastery as early as the year of 1228. The complex, later joined by the church and the monastery building, was placed within city walls because of its location on the East side of the city that was sensitive and busy. It attracted much attention before it was in-

*The Dominican monastery hides a beautiful closed
courtyard and porches that were being built for full 27 years*

cluded in the fortification system due to potential invader attacks. The
church catches the eye due to its simple architecture, and its beauty is
expressed through its closed courtyard and its porches that were being
built full 27 years. The closed interior courtyard was built by domestic
artists Đuro Utišenović and Radovan Grubačević according to the
design by Florence man Maso do Bartolomeo, while the sacristy was

Dominican monastery, five-part painting of Christ's Baptism,
work of Lovro Dobričević, 1448

Dominican monastery, three-part painting, work of Nikola Božidarević

Dominican monastery, Annunciation, work of Nikola Božidarević, 1513

finalized by Paskoje Miličević. The monastery underwent a thorough cosmetic make over during the renaissance period, and it is among other things decorated by an impressive crucifixion located above the main altar that was made 600 years ago, a work of Paolo Venezian from the 14th century, and the altar likeness of St. Magdalene made by Tizian and his assistants. There is also a pretty well crown within the monastery, as well as a bell tower whose construction lasted almost four centuries. The wealth of the monastery also lays in its library that guards numerous documents, manuscripts and inkunables (medieval books, first printed books), yet also the col-lection of works of art dating from the 15th to the 16th century.

Right:
Dominican church,
pictured crucifix by Paolo
Venezian, 14th century

Jesuit Church of St. Ignacio

This is one of the most impressive examples of baroque construction in the region of Dalmatia. It is part of a complex that consists of the Jesuit Church and the Collegium Ragusinum, the Jesuit Academy. This valuable complex appeared on the South side of the Gundulić Field, it continues on with a monumental stairway that leads to the Ruđer Bošković Field -another example of harmony of Dubrovnik's architecture. Devastation of an entire block of old Dubrovnik houses preceded the con-

Interior of The Jesuit Church is decorated by impressive murals

struction of the Jesuit Church and the Academy, and activities regarding purchase, design plans and construction of the complex were finalized as late as the year of 1729.

The church has a richly decorated interior where baroque murals dominate, but a magnificent stairway definitely contributes to its monumental qualities. The stairway is the work of Roman architect Pietro Passalacquo.

Magnificent stairway in front of the Jesuit church

City of harmony and beauty

The Dubrovnik Summer Festival is traditionally held each year

CULTURAL EVENTS
IN DUBROVNIK

Due to their exceptional stone beauty, numerous locations in Dubrovnik are often used as open air stages for a number of cultural manifestations, among which definitely the largest one being the Dubrovnik Summer Festival that are held traditionally each year during July and August.

Stradun nights

This is an international cultural manifestation where music, scenic, and dance ensembles are presented. These are wonderfully harmonized with the primeval scene of this renaissance-baroque city.

In addition, Dubrovnik offers carnival festivities during January, The Karantena Festival or the International Alternative Theater Festival during August and September, the Julian Rachlin and Friends Festival, and an impressive New Year's Eve celebration that is massively held on Stradun and the surrounding squares.

Contents